THE BIRDS, THE RABBITS, THE TREES

Briony Collins is an award-winning writer from North Wales. She manages her time between running *Cape Magazine* and working on her PhD at Bangor University, where she also lectures. Her book, *cactus land*, is forthcoming in 2023 with Atomic Bohemian: her next publishing venture. Currently, Briony resides with her fiancé – Tom – and their mischievous guinea pigs. www.brionycollins.co.uk

Also by Briony Collins

All That Glisters   (Broken Sleep Books, 2022)

Blame it on Me   (Broken Sleep Books, 2021)

The Birds, The Rabbits, The Trees

Briony Collins

Broken Sleep Books

ISBN: 978-1-915760-06-7

Cover designed by Aaron Kent

Edited & Typeset by Aaron Kent

Broken Sleep Books Ltd
Rhydwen
Talgarreg
Ceredigion
SA44 4HB

Broken Sleep Books Ltd
Fair View
St Georges Road
Cornwall
PL26 7YH

Contents

February

Dear Mum,

The forest
Night pouring over unearthed fingers
Beeches reaching from shadows

A vision of your hair
Thrown back from cheeks
Angled, white quartz

Rabbits forage in my black peripheries
Scattering as owls call to each other

Who? Who are you?
You are not here
My dreams grieve you

The unearthed forest
Visions of white fingers
Seventeen years
In black peripheries

What a difference a mother could make

I'm tired of her being dead
That isn't poetic of me, I know
But it's true – I'm tired

Winter morning, winter woman
The days are all outgoing

Instant black coffee and oranges
White veins peel away
She lingers under my nails

I long for her
Lessons on how to love

How to leave
The season rains her absence

Absent

It starts with nothing
A blank page for words

I wake up
The white ceiling
My eyes brim and pour
Into emptiness

Father, father

My insides are so dry
I could drink these tears

I wake up
Don't remember my dreams
My childhood

Clings to cold glass
Liquefies and dribbles down
I could drink these tears

Dad, I wrote for you once
Now only about you
This place is a blank page

Outside these walls
Dew on grass dribbles down
I could

The white ceiling
My childhood
Into emptiness

Charming

My partner is different, not the person
I expected when I was a little girl
We taste like cardamom seeds
Flavour our lives with delicate salivate
But, unsuspecting, rupture vicious fragrance
In the cracks between our teeth
Sometimes my mouth burns
With an unspoken truth
And the words splinter in my jaw
I don't yet know how to say
What I was never prepared to articulate

March

Dear Mum,

Premier Inn, Exeter
Opposite the cathedral
I wake up   [don't recall falling asleep]

Your name in my mouth
Tastes like Malbec

The carpet tickles   [don't recall falling down]
Fibres eel against my cheek

Under the bed, the forest opens
A flicker of light
You?

My boyfriend is shaking me
            What's the matter with you?
                        What the hell?

Opposite the cathedral
God closes his eyes
I wake up

Bitter, purple liquid tangs
My tongue swirls your memory

Your name
A flicker

Cinema

We sit together in muffled dark
Small lights trailing down the aisle like glow worms
Plush red carpet rolling out underfoot
Sometimes gentleness is a warning
They screen our nudity
Make us flinch at the sight of ourselves
Our bodies bent into each other
Flickering into life between scenes
He watches in the white terror of assassination
At the display of beckoning romance
And I with a similar fear
Of the horror between breaths

Nightmare

I stop in the bedroom doorway
Before heading out for the afternoon
It undoes me to watch you sleep
A hairy, half-naked, stench of a creature
Growling viciously as you heave air
Hackles raised at a nightmare
Attacking phantoms behind your eyes
While inside your chest
A heart slows

April

Dear Mum,

In the forest opening
There's a hole
Deep and rectangular

Beech leaves circle the air
Foliage shifting bitter orange
No rabbit or owl sightings
Only echoes

I venture forwards

                              He says I hit my head on the
                              wardrobe

Wind slips past my skin
Dizzy wandering to the edge
I look down
Where are my shoes
There is no fear inside me

You.

Black eyes flung into dead space
Mane settling in the dirt
Blue dress on bone-white body

Your mouth agape
Mid-laugh and full of earth
You'll eat my world alive

He says I never stopped talking
I'm a *schizo* kind of crazy now
Proper funny

Tears salt down my tongues
I am not *there*
I speak to bury myself

Fall next to you
Laugh and swallow the ground
Taste the acridity of rot

A hundred rabbits rush from thickets to us
Thrashing and digging us down until
We are nowhere

The planet vanishes from our backs

Extra-terrestrial

Aren't we all gamblers
He likes lotto cards
And discolouring fists with mandibles

Is it self-harm
If
        I don't know myself

The wall is hard against my skull
Sunlight bleached space-blue carpets
Bright Prawn Nebula

Aren't we all
If
        I stop making any sense

This is the first time
Out of body

        Loosens
Gravity

He holds the top of a Cola bottle
In front of me
Focus on the colour, the shape

Bright Prawn Nebula
On space-blue carpets
The walls are stars

Aren't we all gamblers
Is it self harm

Out of body

Coming out of it

Remember me
I'm forgetting

How I used to occupy
This room this flesh

More always more
Always forgetting
Remember

I catch her inset
Four-cornered silver eye
Blinks back

Face like a pufferfish
White bracken underbelly
Lips mid-scream wide

There were tears once
Some way of telling

How I used to
Remember this flesh

May

Dear Mum,

A schizo kind of crazy now
Your name in my fever
Seventeen years

> *The birds, the rabbits, the trees*
> *That's all you said,* he told me

The crack in the ceiling paint
Above my bed
Is shaped like the River Nile
An ibis drinks

> *The birds*

I can see Thebes
I vomit

Proper funny
I laugh

> *The rabbits*

My tonsils bubble with pus
Sweat wrings out of me like a wet towel
The doctor gave me penicillin

I can see Thebes
No tomb for me
Just a hole in a forest

The trees

An ambulance arrives
I curse them for making me late

Notes from the other side

Have I lived something stupid? Am I the coward responsible for nothing?
— Forrest Gander, *Be With*

There, a lingering blink of Solstice
Shade on the hottest day of the year
The summer is ending

Kiss me golden
Before

I dream of water
Seeping vitality from sweat glands
My insides are pot pourri

I dream of copper
Basking warm and ascending blue
Like the roof of the bell tower at primary school

Ms Bartlett told me I couldn't cry forever
We all run out of current one day

I dream of soil
Retaining me, blooming me from soft flesh
And then, silently, waiting

Take my hand
Before

I shut my eyes and there is nothing

Petrichor

All I know now is this smell
Humid musk of a week in the salted dark
Sweat pressed into sheets like a permanent shadow
Bile from the pit of my stomach retched into every corner

Argillaceous odour of the coming night
I wear death like perfume dabbed on delicate skin
My wrists, my clavicle, my aching neck
I am scented for the season

June

Dear Mum,

After I'm discharged
From the hospital
I wait for you in the forest
You don't come
You're afraid of ghosts

I want to tell you
That I understand
The fear doesn't last
Vicious lucidity numbs to velvet

That's the way it went
For you

Last Request

I'm scared to be new
That's why I stay

I don't have the energy
To open myself again

How many

Hello / How are you / What do you do for a living / How do you
spend your free time / Shall we get out of here / Let's go back to my
place / The fog descending / The clothes rustling / The flesh / The
ashes / The silence –

Should I die here
Don't come to my funeral

Grief is exhausting
My body is ancient

Just stand in the doorway
And pour out a drink

Maybe I'll catch it
On my way out

Do I

The window above the kitchen sink is open
Our new flat is in the basement
The ground above us
A white cat sits at shoulder-height and stares through the glass
At the crying woman doing the dishes
The air down here is ectoplasm
Muggy and hard to fill lungs with
If I shut the window I will die
The ground above me
A white cat speaks: *come, come outside and play*
The dishes won't wash themselves
If I go outside I will die

July

Dear Mum,

The time when I knew you is lost
How much can I write to a stranger

You told your friend about my birth
In a letter I found last week

> *I don't think I've ever been so scared*

There is no fear in our forest
The time when you knew me is lost

I have visions of breaking my thumbs
Leave them hanging on by nothing

But bloody, finger-picked skin
So I don't have to hit the spacebar again

I'm sick of spaces

The implication of more to say
When we are robbed of words

> *The birds, the rabbits, the trees*

The planet vanishes from our backs
I violate myself

In Memory

She picks daisies that match the ones on her pink sandals, pierces their stems with an index nail, threads them together into a chain the way my love for her is threaded into veins. She is stitched into me with blood, a string of red youth embroidering me with its colour.

My daughter, she is dead. My daughter, she was never here.

The flowers run out, so I bury her to bloom fresh in her decay, but I do not kill. *A man met her, unspooled her innocence then unpicked the tacks from my insides to have more of her.* There are no other words for it: she is undone so I engulf her, hear her drumming on

the underside of this life: *my mother, I am you.*

No more

Last night
I had a panic attack
in the shower

The water crested
over my face
and I became it

I crashed and sang
against the plastic
bottles in the corner

the mildew
growing underneath
the shampoo

I left my skin
as steam, clung
to the ceiling, tiles

to the glass door
where I splashed
and trickled

toward the drain
I span in circles
dizzied myself

on metal
I disappeared
down

August

Dear Mum,

He watches me
        with intent

My knuckles want to split my skin
How do I stop the burst of bone through flesh
The birth of a skeletal truth

    I don't think I've ever been so scared

His eyes are malice black
Pupil folds seize a cryptid glare
The stare of a creature hunting

I flee to the forest
He's always around the corner
Foraging in peripheries

    What's the matter with you? What the hell?

Vicious lucidity numbs to velvet
I'm not *there*
How far can he chase a stranger

In the forest opening, there's a hole
I climb inside to hide
He'll eat my world alive

After a drink

Your shark eyes,
with their transparent lid-glaze
over hunting pupils,
track the slow scent
of quarter-mile old blood
flagging in the deep.

Cryptid

[The hitchhiker thumbs in the dark]

He's all yellow eyes and deadlife
Headlights firing into highway nights

He knows: I'm worth nothing
The barren core of a tunnel

[The hitchhiker enters]

Unfastens belts and succeeds
Inside arterial fear

This necrosis of woman
Betrays me in a layby

[The hitchhiker grins]

The fixed visage of Grendel
But I'm the one unarmed

All yellow eyes
I'll never get off this highway alive

September

Dear Mum,

Insects nestle in the smooth alcoves of my eye sockets
Roots tangle themselves around fragments of my skull
Finger skin is coming undone in wet, white ribbons

The forest is omnipresent night

He looks different in daylight; a boy with full cheeks
Not the gaunt flesh the moon hollows into bone
How do I stop a skeletal truth

I don't feel alive anymore

Epiphany

*Is it a right thing or a mad thing not to want to re-connect, to avoid
reading or writing because of what those will bring?*
– Bhanu Kapil, *Schizophrene*

Evenings pass inside a wine glass
The pour and swill of distant warmth
I heave tannins

On a shelf in our flat
A journal contains you
To touch it is to burn

Nightly I stare
At its hard spine and unflayed skin
A mirror

An epiphany against death
I'd live any life but this one

Marginal Glosses

the way
mosses
bulge in
cement
around
bricks: a
portmanteau

love is
only real
if it is
mutual

[POEM]

we are all
moss, all
subtext;
i don't
have the
right words
for you

and now
you'll never
read me
again

October

Mummy,

On a grey street in Abergavenny
My boyfriend looks the other way

His friend swirls sweaty, cig-stained fingers up my thigh
Tracing along and under my skirt

The birds, the rabbits, the trees

In a room full of men, nobody speaks
My body strains to laugh it off

Proper funny

There's a wedding tomorrow
My dress is the misty blue of Anglesey at dawn

The groomsmen are drunk, riotous
A friend of my partner is a friend of mine

Beeches reaching from shadows

I am safe I am I am I am

The birds, the rabbits, the trees

I am running upstairs crying I am I
The birds, the rabbits, the trees
Like migraines make me vomit without nausea not for a second
I know I'm sick when I'm throwing up I am already up upstairs I am
Shaking the tears the tears the tears *the birds, the rabbits, the trees*

the tears are worse when my boyfriend follows

> "You're making a fucking scene
> > You always do this
> > > I didn't even see anything
> > > > I'm done with you"

On a grey street in Abergavenny
I look the other way

The forest takes me

Here is your fucking scene

We were there for your friend's wedding
when the best man groped me the night before.

So I didn't behave like I should when I ran upstairs crying,
because he was still your mate after all.

Instead I should have palm-heeled his nose into the back of his
brain, sent shards into his skull until violence poured from nostrils.
I should have called you the name I was thinking and spat in your
black eyes, black like the coffee I drowned in the next morning
because I stayed up until dawn in the black room, watching black
shadows move against the black wall where I waited like a fly in
the corner for him to return and eviscerate me, all legs and eyes,
finishing what he started.

I should have grabbed the beer bottle on the table and crowned him
with the broken pieces of an unconscionable statistic – *one in five
women* – and then I should have kicked him after he slumped on the
floor, six feet closer to Hell.

So I didn't behave like I should when I shut myself in the bedroom,
while you yelled at me through the door for making a scene.

Or all the next day when we went to the ceremony and you told me
that you loved me, that one day it would be us promising each other
eternity, and the bride told me at the reception not to mind him
because that's just what he's like, and that bitch at our table told me
if I wasn't so passive it wouldn't have happened.

So I didn't behave like I should, but in my head I nicked the cigarillos
from your coat pocket, went outside to light one up,

then set the whole building on fire too, waiting for sirens,
for screams, for the blaze of my heart to die.

Fantasy

I hope you read this one day and find a cold shard of a memory
that, even though I never wrote your name, you recognise
and it cuts you.

November

Dear Mum,

He lifts the debit card from my purse and takes the train to Prestatyn
Treating himself to a pack of John Smiths and cigarillos on the way

I lie on the sofa and pull the blanket over my head
I'm in a coffin; a true Rosencrantz

You glimmer like a gymnast wrapped in silks, your spiritual trapeze
Suspended from the branches inside my head

My hands strike reverberations through shadows to your spotlight
Or lay still at my side on the pleather couch

I don't know

How to recognise when love dies
Though your voice is gone, I spend my life in your forest

While another mutates and withers on a train
Can anyone new love me while I lie in a box

Even when I'm in a real coffin they'll say
Bless her heart, she's gone back to her mother at last

The phone call

...with his stupid Bundy black eyes...
Meg is saying through the phone
and I laugh because it's true.

The carpet under my fingernails is grimy,
glittery with the mucous of the slugs
that come in through the hole behind the tumble dryer.
That must be how my face looks,
trails and stains and oils,
the sluggish, viscous jelly of my nose.

...I never liked him...
and I don't think I did either.
Sometimes, by the time you love someone, you forget to check.
My lungs heave mildew and dust mites,
blacken the back of my throat with mould,
spore white on convulsing tonsils.

It's true: I am overripe.
My days come and go until I slip
from slime to fluff to slime again,
disease-riddled and poisonous.
...Pirate-looking motherfucker with his scurvy and his stench...
I laugh and jump at the sound of myself,

then jump again as he storms through the door,
never having left in the first place,
but squatting outside with his ear to the wood,
waiting.

It makes you so sick

Eat away my linings
        Break me in enzymes
                Reclaim me in acid

As a kid I collected woodlice in an empty margarine tub
Until Grandma said they'd revolt, swarm me, devour me

                I crawl up our walls
        Beetle into corners
Scuttle in the dark

I almost set the box alight, ended their coup at the root
The worst pause of my life as I held the match up

How does it feel
        That I chose to come
                But not to stay

You could keep me in this flat and feed on me forever
Or burn this place up real good to stop

                The infestation
        Digging her way
Out

December

Dear Mum,

I almost killed someone
He said

Anger is white

It splits me open like the frantic froth of a waterfall
A current spilling from a ledge
Punching into the gaping body beneath
Writhing in its own tide

The white is on me when I cry
His pupils set into the frozen snow of his sclerae
Deathly, deadly, searing
Like his white fist cut into the temple of an old man

His ankle cracks as he twists and storms out

I feel you bandage your fingers around mine
Lead me to the forest

In the moonlit clearing is the hole
Where I first found it in the spring

Rabbits flank us, swarm our heels but never overtake
Wings of owls brush through the air

Your arms are all tremors and gooseflesh
Squeeze my hand harder

Face the chasm and stepping
We fall beyond the sounds of the birds, the rabbits, the trees

The open grave of my mind
Where I meet you every night of my life

Seeds

Do abusers ever believe they are justified? When they take a life between their hands and compress it, squeeze it between their palms until they can mould it like clay? Do they think that because the marks they leave are on the mind no barbarity has occurred? How many women are faced with these questions?

The first time I tried to leave, you curled up on the bedroom floor and cried: *they won, they won*, as though the world sought to steal me away. How far gone was I to not see the violence of those words, the preconception of war instilled in me by the rhetoric of battle? That words, though not the cause of physical assault, are the seeds of it?

You planted a seed a long time ago. *It's you and me versus the world.* It germinated in me, sprouted up as a tendril in my mind, pushed through the soil of my scalp and out into the garden of my external self. You nurtured your protection inside me. How could I live as a deserter? Cowardice is worthy of execution.

What is real

Beyond the forest is a lake
where water snakes buckle in boat wakes
and mothers, eggless, jelly their young
direct into the dark pool

I drown into being
the living swim in the ridges of my brain
no time for flinching; I rise
the lake pours itself into day

January

Dear Mum,

My dreams grieve you
Almost eighteen years

I pack his things for him
Proper funny

Sweat wrings out of him like a wet towel
I laugh

My mouth full of earth
I'll eat his world alive

The first night is quiet
The birth of a skeletal truth

I'm going to be okay

Pussy

It's just another word you throw around because there is nothing so weak, so chickenshit to you as womanhood, nothing like shrugging off blood and the glide of wet muscle to prove how much power you have, how the comparison of your mates to femininity is laughable, is worth only a cheap comment for a fist bump in the pub at all our expense, and these are only the women with vaginas but truthfully you hate the lot of us.

You can think of nothing so demeaning as the space between a pair of legs that could bring you home again, but anyone who isn't as rough as you, isn't armed with bark and cigars, cocksure in decay and sinking whisky, well, they're a fucking pussy, but even so it's you curled up on the sofa now, making one last plea while I pack and know you don't understand the meaning of the word. You couldn't begin to comprehend the strength of it.

You know who you are

This is the last time I write about you.

And I don't give a fuck if it's too straight,
if these lines cut into paper and don't bleed
because there's no heart left underneath.

      Besides, I never bled either

when you sunk another
      whisky and wondered why it turned
      the tributaries of your eyes to venom,
then you drilled a fist
      into a lamppost, glowering in amber,
      the vision of my face caught on metal,
my breath; rainclouds.

And I don't give a fuck if the words won't bloom,
won't speak in petals that layer each other
with grace and delicacy and subtext.

      We never had any of that.

We were all entrails,
      you wanted viscera instead of woman;
      ancient haruspicy in the pools of my organs.
How many ways are
      there to dissect a human being? We were
      all insides – yellow livers and black lungs,
intestines pink as lips.

And I don't give a fuck if it's the worst
thing I've ever written – maybe there's still

a place for bad poems like bad people. Hell,

       I'll meet you there

just to watch you die
       unalive, searing – your pupils were black
       as you came through the door grinning:
Briony, Briony, I think
       I killed him, and you smiled like a little boy
       waiting for golden praise and silver laughter,
to be sung to like a chime.

And I don't give a fuck if this poem undoes you,
you didn't have to hit him, didn't have to leave
him unmoving on the stone slabs outside the pub,

       didn't have to come back
to break me one last time –
       those hands that touched me
turned skulls to stars:
           fragments of fire,
                burning of bone,
                     sights set to solar flares,

       and you,
          beaming.

Acknowledgements

Before I extend my gratitude to people, I would like to highlight my use of the word 'schizo' in *The Birds, The Rabbits, The Trees*. Each time it is used, I am quoting what my ex said to me. His use of the word is harmful, as it reinforces stereotypes and fails to consider the breadth of experiences people living with schizophrenia undergo. I made the artistic decision to include it to record his behaviour and wanted to include a note acknowledging this choice here.

I would like to thank the amazing people from Bangor University who have encouraged and helped me over the years, but especially with this book: James Wilkes, Fiona Cameron, and Zoë Skoulding. Without them, this book would not exist.

I am grateful to all my friends for their endless support, but particularly to Aaron Farrell and Anna Monnereau for always motivating me to keep going.

My family, as always, are the source of my strength. Especially Tom, who has shown me what real love feels like, and helps me to be a stronger person every day.

Lastly, I want to thank myself. For being brave. For standing up. For putting myself first.

This book is dedicated to me.

LAY OUT YOUR UNREST

www.ingramcontent.com/pod-product-compliance
Lightning Source LLC
Chambersburg PA
CBHW021943040426
42448CB00008B/1222